the tree

the cat

the bird

The bird is up in the tree.

The cat is near the tree.

The cat looks up.
He sees the bird
in the tree.

The little bird is singing up in the tree.

The cat runs to the tree.

He jumps up into the tree.
He climbs up and up and up.

As the cat climbs up
the little bird looks down.
She looks at the cat.

The cat sits very still.
He is on a branch.

The little bird is afraid of the cat.

The big cat jumps
from the branch.

The bird flies up
out of the tree.

Little robin redbreast
sat upon a tree.
Up went pussycat
and down went he.
Down came pussy
and away robin ran.
Said little robin redbreast
catch me if you can.